APPLES
Cookbook

Copyright © 2012 CQ Products
Waverly, IA 50677
All rights reserved.
No part of this book may be reproduced or transmitted in any form or by any means, electronic or mechanical, including photocopying, recording or by any information storage and retrieval system, without permission in writing from the publisher, CQ Products.

Printed in the USA by G&R Publishing Co., Waverly, IA

Published and distributed by:

CQ Products

507 Industrial Street
Waverly, IA 50677

ISBN-13: 978-1-56383-428-8
ISBN-10: 1-56383-428-6
Item #3726

Choosing the Best Apples

When purchasing apples, look for:
- firm texture
- smooth bright skin with no bruises, worm holes or punctures
- intact stems
- apples that feel heavy for their size
- apple-like aroma

Storage tips
- Store unwashed whole apples in a cool dry place or in a ventilated plastic bag in the refrigerator for 4 to 6 weeks.
- Keep apples away from onions and garlic.
- To prevent browning of sliced apples, dip into lemon or orange juice and refrigerate in an airtight container. Anti-browning products may also be used.

Type of apples to buy
Textures vary from crisp to soft and flavors range from tart to sweet, making some apples better for cooking and others better for fresh eating. When baking or cooking

with apples, try combining several different types for richer flavor. The following suggestions will offer excellent results, but personal preferences and availability will help you choose which apples to use in each recipe.

All-purpose apples, equally good for fresh eating, cooking and baking: Braeburn, Cameo, Cortland, Empire, Golden Delicious, Granny Smith, Gravenstein, Honeycrisp, Jonathan, McIntosh, Newton, Paula Red, Spartan

Especially good for fresh eating: Ambrosia, Crimson Gold, Crispin, Fuji, Gala, Ginger Gold, Honeycrisp, Jonagold, Jonamac, Pink Lady, Red Delicious, Spartan

Especially good for applesauce: Cameo, Cortland, Crispin, Fuji, Gala, Ida Red, Lodi, Macoun, McIntosh, Melrose, Pippin, Rome, Winesap

Especially good for pies and baked desserts: Cortland, Gala, Gravenstein, Haralson, Honeycrisp, Ida Red, Macoun, Northern Spy, Pink Lady, Pippin, Rome, Stayman, Wealthy

Especially good for baking whole (to retain shape): Crispin, Macoun, Rhode Island Greening, Rome, Winesap

Especially good for cider and juices: Baldwin, Gala, Golden Russet, Grimes Golden, Honeycrisp, Jonagold, Wealthy, Winesap

Flavor profiles
  Slightly to Very Tart: Cameo, Granny Smith, Gravenstein, Haralson, Ida Red, Jonamac, Macoun, Northern Spy, Paula Red, Pippin, Winesap
  Tart-Sweet: Empire, Fuji, Honeycrisp, Jonagold, Jonathan, Pink Lady, McIntosh
  Sweet: Baldwin, Braeburn, Cortland, Crispin, Criterion, Fuji, Gala, Golden Delicious, Red Delicious, Rome

Other helpful tips:
- One pound of apples is approximately 2 large, 3 medium or 4 small apples.
- One medium apple equals about 1 cup sliced or ⅔ cup chopped apple.
- It takes about 7 medium apples to make one 9″ pie.
- When cooking with apples, increase sweetness by adding a little sugar; increase tartness with a few drops of lemon juice.
- For the best flavor, use a combination of sweet and tart apples in pies, sauces and other baked or cooked dishes.
- Choose firm, crisp apples for freezing; choose softer apples for applesauce.
- Unless stated otherwise, recipes in this book call for medium-size apples.

Appetizers & Snacks

Creamy Toffee Crunch Dip

1 (8 oz.) pkg. cream cheese, softened
¼ C. sugar
½ C. brown sugar
1 tsp. vanilla extract

½ (8 oz.) pkg. toffee bits, divided
2 red apples, any variety
2 green apples, any variety
Orange juice or fruit preservative

In a medium bowl, mix cream cheese, sugar, brown sugar and vanilla until creamy and well blended. Stir in most of the toffee bits. Place in a serving bowl and sprinkle remaining toffee bits over top. Core and slice apples; dip in orange juice to prevent browning. Drain well before serving. Serve dip with apple slices. Makes 8 to 10 servings.

Cheddar-Apple Pie Dip

¼ C. brown sugar
¼ tsp. ground cinnamon
1 C. chopped red apple, any variety
1 C. chopped green apple, any variety
½ C. chopped walnuts

1 (8 oz.) pkg. cream cheese, softened
½ C. sour cream
1½ C. shredded sharp Cheddar cheese
Wheat crackers

Preheat oven to 375°. In a medium bowl, combine brown sugar and cinnamon. Add red and green apples and walnuts; toss until evenly coated and set aside. In another medium bowl, mix cream cheese, sour cream and Cheddar cheese until well blended. Spread cheese mixture in a 9″ pie plate. Top with apple mixture. Bake for 20 minutes or until heated through. Serve with crackers. Makes 12 to 15 servings.

Chicken-Apple Stuffed Tomatoes

About 30 cherry tomatoes
1 Granny Smith apple, peeled and cored
1 tsp. lemon juice
1 C. finely chopped cooked chicken breast, chilled
Salt and pepper to taste

¼ tsp. ground cinnamon
1½ T. mayonnaise
1 tsp. chopped fresh parsley
Small parsley sprigs for garnish, optional

Cut off a small slice from the top of each tomato; use a melon baller or small spoon to scoop out seeds. Place tomato shells upside down on paper towels to drain for 10 minutes. Meanwhile, shred or dice apple into a medium bowl; toss with lemon juice to coat. Add chicken, salt, pepper, cinnamon, mayonnaise and chopped parsley; stir well. Fill tomato shells generously with chicken mixture and garnish with parsley sprigs, if desired. Serve promptly. Makes about 30 tomatoes.

Battered Apple & Onion Rings

Excellent! Everyone loved the apples for desert & onions w/ dinner. 9/15

2 T. ground cinnamon
3 T. sugar
1 tsp. salt, divided, plus extra for sprinkling
1 egg white
1 C. beer

1 C. flour
Vegetable oil for frying
3 Granny Smith apples, peeled and cored
1 large onion, ends trimmed and skin removed

In a small bowl, mix cinnamon, sugar and ½ teaspoon salt; reserve for later use. In a medium bowl, whisk egg white until frothy. Stir in beer. Whisk in flour and ½ teaspoon salt until batter is smooth; set aside. In a deep-fryer or deep heavy saucepan, heat about 2″ of oil to 375°. Meanwhile, slice each apple into five rings and pat dry with paper towels. Cut onion into ½″ slices and separate into rings. One ring at a time, dip apples into batter and allow excess to drip off. Place in hot oil and fry apple rings for 1 to 2 minutes on each side until golden brown. Remove from oil and drain on paper towels. Dip, fry and drain onion rings the same way. Sprinkle apple rings with reserved cinnamon mixture. Sprinkle onion rings with salt. Serve promptly. Makes 6 to 8 servings.

Gala Egg Rolls

4 Gala apples
2 T. butter
2 T. brown sugar
1 tsp. ground cinnamon

12 egg roll wrappers
Vegetable oil for frying
Powdered sugar

Peel, core and finely chop apples; set aside. In a medium skillet over medium heat, melt butter. Stir in brown sugar and cinnamon until blended. Add apples and stir to coat; cook until softened, 3 to 4 minutes. Remove from heat. Divide apple mixture between egg roll wrappers. Roll up and seal edges with a little water as needed, following package directions. In a deep-fryer or deep heavy saucepan, heat about 3" of oil to 375°. Fry egg rolls for 1 to 2 minutes or until golden brown on all sides. Remove from oil and drain on paper towels. Dust with powdered sugar before serving. Makes 12 egg rolls.

Jazzed-Up Deviled Eggs

1 T. butter
2 green onions, finely chopped
½ Jazz or Granny Smith apple, cored and diced
1 tsp. chopped fresh parsley

6 hard-cooked eggs, cooled
2 T. mayonnaise
½ tsp. Dijon mustard
Salt and pepper to taste
Paprika, optional

In a small skillet over medium heat, melt butter. Add onions and sauté for 2 minutes. Add apple and cook 1 minute longer. Remove from heat and stir in parsley; let cool. Meanwhile, peel off egg shells and slice each egg in half lengthwise. Remove yolks and place in a shallow bowl; mash well. Stir in mayonnaise, Dijon mustard, apple mixture, salt and pepper until well blended. Spoon a portion of filling mixture into each egg white half; sprinkle with paprika, if desired. Serve promptly or cover and chill. Makes 12 eggs.

Apple-Mango Salsa

1 Granny Smith or other tart apple
1 tsp. plus 2 T. lime juice, divided
1 ripe firm mango
¼ C. diced red onion
1 tomato, seeded and diced
1 jalapeño pepper, seeded and minced
2 T. chopped fresh mint
Salt and pepper to taste

Peel, core and dice apple into a medium bowl; toss with 1 teaspoon lime juice. Peel, core and dice mango; add to bowl with apple. Add onion, tomato and jalapeño; toss together gently. Add mint, remaining 2 tablespoons lime juice, salt and pepper; stir until well combined. Cover and refrigerate at least 1 hour or overnight. Serve with pita or tortilla chips, on fish or meat dishes or with tacos. Makes 12 to 15 servings.

Peanut Butter-Bacon Applewiches

6 to 8 bacon strips
½ C. peanut butter
1 red apple, any variety, cored

1 T. lemon juice
8 slices bread, toasted

In a skillet or microwave, cook bacon until crisp; drain on paper towels and crumble into a small bowl. Add peanut butter and mix well; set aside. Quarter and slice apple into 16 wedges. Toss apple slices with lemon juice; drain well. To assemble, divide peanut butter mixture evenly among bread slices and spread smoothly. Arrange apple slices over peanut butter on half the bread slices; top with remaining bread slices. Cut sandwiches in half, if desired. Makes 4 sandwiches.

Broiled Apple Toast

4 tsp. butter, softened
4 slices whole wheat bread

1 apple, any variety
1 T. ground cinnamon

Set oven to broil. Spread about 1 teaspoon butter on one side of each slice of bread. Core and thinly slice apple. Arrange apple slices evenly on buttered side of bread slices. Sprinkle some cinnamon over apple slices. Place bread on an ungreased broiler pan, apple side up. Broil for 1 to 2 minutes or until toasted. Makes 4 sandwiches.

Dried Cinnamon Apple Chips

2 C. unsweetened apple juice
1 cinnamon stick

2 Red Delicious or other sweet apples

Preheat oven to 250°. Lightly spray wire racks with nonstick cooking spray; set aside. In a large saucepan over medium-low heat, combine apple juice and cinnamon stick. Bring to a low boil. Meanwhile, remove apple stems and cut apples crosswise into ⅛"-thick slices; discard the top and bottom slices. Place slices into boiling juice; cook for 4 to 5 minutes or until apples become translucent and slightly golden. Drain on paper towels; pat dry. Arrange slices on prepared wire racks, without touching or overlapping. Place on center rack in oven to bake for 30 to 40 minutes or until lightly browned and almost dry to the touch. Check several times during baking to prevent overbrowning. Remove from oven and let cool completely. Store in an airtight container. If storing longer than 2 days, refrigerate. Makes about 40 chips.

Breads & Brunch

Mini Apple Muffins

- 2 C. flour
- ½ C. sugar
- 1 T. baking powder
- 1 tsp. ground cinnamon
- ½ tsp. salt

- ¾ C. apple juice
- 1 egg, lightly beaten
- ⅓ C. vegetable oil
- 1 C. peeled, finely diced apple, any variety

Preheat oven to 400°. Grease bottoms of 36 mini muffin cups or line with paper liners. In a medium bowl, stir together flour, sugar, baking powder, cinnamon and salt. In a large bowl, whisk together apple juice, egg and oil. Add dry ingredients and stir until just moistened but still lumpy. Stir in apple. Divide batter among prepared muffin cups, filling each cup about ⅔ full. Bake for 10 to 14 minutes or until a toothpick inserted near center comes out clean. Cool for 1 minute before removing from pan. Serve warm. Makes 36 mini muffins.

Note: You may also make 12 standard muffins and bake them for 18 to 22 minutes.

Streusel-Topped Pumpkin Muffins

2½ C. plus 2 T. flour, divided
2¼ C. sugar, divided
1 T. ground pumpkin pie spice
1 tsp. baking soda
½ tsp. salt
2 eggs, lightly beaten

½ C. vegetable oil
1 C. canned pumpkin puree
2 C. peeled, chopped apples, any variety
½ tsp. ground cinnamon
4 tsp. butter

Preheat oven to 350°. Lightly grease 18 muffin cups or line with paper liners. In a large bowl, whisk together 2½ cups flour, 2 cups sugar, pumpkin pie spice, baking soda and salt. In a separate bowl, whisk together eggs, oil and pumpkin; add to flour mixture and stir until just moistened. Fold in apples. Divide batter among prepared muffin cups, filling each cup about ⅔ full; set aside. In a small bowl, mix remaining 2 tablespoons flour, remaining ¼ cup sugar and cinnamon. With a pastry blender or two knives, cut in butter until mixture is crumbly. Sprinkle cinnamon mixture evenly over batter in each cup. Bake for 35 to 40 minutes or until a toothpick inserted in center comes out clean. Makes 18 muffins.

Apple-Blueberry Muffins

2 C. flour
½ C. sugar
1 T. baking powder
½ tsp. salt
½ tsp. ground cinnamon
1 tsp. lemon zest

1 C. milk
1 egg, lightly beaten
⅓ C. vegetable oil
½ C. fresh blueberries
1 C. peeled, chopped apples, any variety
Sugar for sprinkling

Preheat oven to 400°. Grease 12 muffin cups or line with paper liners; set aside. In a large bowl, stir together flour, sugar, baking powder, salt, cinnamon and lemon zest until combined. In a small bowl, whisk together milk, egg and oil until well blended. Make a well in the center of flour mixture and pour in milk mixture; stir until just moistened but still lumpy. Gently fold in blueberries and apples. Divide batter among prepared muffin cups, filling each cup about ¾ full. Sprinkle tops lightly with sugar. Bake for 20 to 25 minutes or until golden brown. Serve promptly. Makes 12 muffins.

Sweet Apple Fritters

Vegetable oil for frying
2 C. biscuit baking mix
1 egg, lightly beaten
¼ C. sugar

1 tsp. ground cinnamon
1¾ C. chopped Granny Smith apples
¼ C. powdered sugar

In a deep-fryer or deep heavy saucepan, heat about 3˝ of oil to 350°. Meanwhile, in a large bowl, combine baking mix, ½ cup water, egg, sugar and cinnamon; stir to blend. Fold in apples. Working in small batches, drop batter by tablespoonfuls into hot oil. Cook for 2 to 3 minutes or until golden brown, turning occasionally. Remove fritters from oil and drain on paper towels. Before serving, sprinkle with powdered sugar. Makes about 32 fritters.

Apple Nut Bread

2 C. flour
1 tsp. baking powder
½ tsp. baking soda
½ tsp. salt
½ C. chopped walnuts

½ C. butter, softened
1 C. sugar
2 eggs, lightly beaten
1 tsp. vanilla extract
1 C. peeled, shredded apple, any variety

Preheat oven to 350°. Grease a 5 x 9˝ loaf pan; set aside. In a medium bowl, combine flour, baking powder, baking soda, salt and walnuts. In a large mixing bowl, beat together butter, sugar and one egg until smooth. Beat in remaining egg and vanilla until blended. Stir in apple. Add flour mixture to apple mixture and stir until just moistened. Spread in prepared pan. Bake for 50 to 60 minutes or until a toothpick inserted in center comes out clean. Let stand 10 minutes before removing from pan to cool completely on a wire rack. Makes 1 loaf.

Note: If desired, stir 1 tablespoon lemon zest into batter and drizzle warm bread with a glaze made from lemon juice and powdered sugar.

Apple-Zucchini Bread

1 C. peeled, shredded Granny Smith apple
1 C. finely grated zucchini
1¼ C. brown sugar
1 C. vegetable oil
3 eggs
1 tsp. vanilla extract

3 C. plus ½ tsp. flour, divided
¼ tsp. salt
1½ tsp. baking powder
1½ tsp. baking soda
1 tsp. ground cinnamon
1 tsp. ground nutmeg
1 C. chopped pecans

Preheat oven to 375°. Grease two 4½ x 8½" loaf pans. Line with parchment paper and grease the paper; set aside. In a large bowl, combine apple, zucchini, brown sugar, oil, eggs and vanilla; mix well. In another bowl, stir together 3 cups flour, salt, baking powder, baking soda, cinnamon and nutmeg. Add flour mixture to apple mixture and stir well to blend. In a resealable plastic bag, combine pecans with remaining ½ teaspoon flour; seal and shake to coat pecans. Stir pecans into batter until well incorporated. Divide batter between prepared pans. Bake for 50 to 60 minutes or until a toothpick inserted in center comes out clean. Let stand several minutes before removing from pans to cool on a wire rack. Makes 2 loaves.

Apple Scones

2 C. flour
¼ C. plus 2 T. sugar, divided
2 tsp. baking powder
½ tsp. baking soda
½ tsp. salt

¼ C. butter, chilled
1 apple, any variety
½ C. plus 2 T. milk, divided
¾ tsp. ground cinnamon

Preheat oven to 425°. Lightly grease a baking sheet; set aside. In a large bowl, combine flour, ¼ cup sugar, baking powder, baking soda and salt; mix well. With a pastry blender or two knives, cut in butter until crumbly. Peel and shred apple; add apple and ½ cup milk to flour mixture and stir until soft dough forms. Place on a lightly floured surface and knead 8 to 10 times. Pat dough into two 6″ circles and set on prepared baking sheet, leaving space between them. Brush tops with remaining 2 tablespoons milk. Sprinkle with remaining 2 tablespoons sugar and cinnamon. With knife or pizza cutter, score each circle into six pie-shaped wedges. Bake for 15 minutes or until lightly browned and puffy. Serve warm with butter. Makes 12 scones.

Apple-Cheese Bread

½ C. butter, softened
⅔ C. sugar
2 eggs
2 C. flour
1 tsp. baking powder
½ tsp. baking soda

½ tsp. salt
1½ C. peeled, shredded apples, any variety
½ C. shredded Cheddar cheese
1 C. chopped almonds, pecans or walnuts

Preheat oven to 350°. Grease a 5 x 9" loaf pan and set aside. In a large mixing bowl, beat together butter and sugar until light and creamy. Beat in eggs. In a separate bowl, whisk together flour, baking powder, baking soda and salt. Add flour mixture to creamed mixture and beat until blended. Fold in apples, cheese and almonds. Spread batter in prepared pan. Bake for 55 to 60 minutes or until top springs back when pressed lightly. Cool on a wire rack before removing from pan. Makes 1 loaf.

Apple Coffee Cake

2 C. flaked wheat bran cereal
1 C. flour
1½ tsp. baking powder
2 tsp. ground cinnamon, divided
Dash of ground nutmeg
¼ tsp. salt
¼ C. butter, softened

¾ C. plus 2 T. sugar, divided
2 egg whites
1 tsp. vanilla extract
¼ C. milk
1½ C. peeled, chopped apples, any variety

Preheat oven to 375°. Grease an 8 x 8″ baking pan and set aside. In a medium bowl, stir together cereal, flour, baking powder, 1 teaspoon cinnamon, nutmeg and salt. In a large mixing bowl, beat butter and ¾ cup sugar until well blended. Add egg whites and vanilla; beat until smooth. Beat in half the cereal mixture; add milk and beat well. Beat in remaining cereal mixture. Stir in apples until blended. Spread batter in prepared pan. In a small bowl, stir together remaining 2 tablespoons sugar and remaining 1 teaspoon cinnamon. Sprinkle sugar mixture over batter. Bake for 25 minutes or until a toothpick inserted in center comes out clean. Makes 12 servings.

Country Apple Biscuit Bake

1½ C. peeled, chopped apples,
  any variety, divided
1 (12 oz.) tube refrigerated flaky biscuits
2 T. butter, softened
⅓ C. brown sugar
¼ tsp. ground cinnamon
⅓ C. light corn syrup

1 egg
1½ tsp. whiskey, optional
½ C. pecan halves
⅓ C. powdered sugar
1 tsp. vanilla extract
1 to 2 tsp. milk

Preheat oven to 350°. Grease a 9" round baking pan and add 1 cup apples, spreading evenly. Separate dough into 10 biscuits; cut each biscuit into four even pieces. Arrange biscuit pieces, points up, over apples. Top with remaining ½ cup apples; set aside. In a small bowl, combine butter, brown sugar, cinnamon, corn syrup, egg and whiskey, if desired. Beat for 2 to 3 minutes or until sugar is partially dissolved. Stir in pecans. Spoon mixture over biscuits and apples. Bake for 35 to 45 minutes or until deep golden brown. Cool for 5 minutes before removing from pan. To make glaze, whisk together powdered sugar, vanilla and enough milk to make a drizzling consistency. Drizzle mixture over warm cake. Serve warm or cool. Makes 8 servings.

Apple Pinwheel Rolls

⅓ C. butter, softened
1 C. sugar
3 C. peeled, finely chopped tart apples, any variety

3 T. brown sugar
1 tsp. ground apple pie spice
2 (8 oz.) tubes refrigerated seamless crescent dough sheets

Preheat oven to 350°. Grease a 10 x 15" jellyroll pan; set aside. In a small saucepan over medium heat, combine ⅓ cup water, butter and sugar. Cook until butter is melted and sugar dissolves; remove from heat and let syrup stand. Meanwhile, drain apples and place in a large bowl. Add brown sugar and apple pie spice; toss to coat and set aside. On waxed paper, unroll one dough sheet. Spread half of apple mixture over dough to within 1" of edges. Starting at one long side, roll up jellyroll-style, using waxed paper to assist with rolling. Pinch long edges to seal. Cut into 1" slices and place in prepared pan. Repeat with remaining dough sheet and filling. Pour prepared syrup over rolls. Bake for 40 to 45 minutes or until golden brown. Serve warm. Makes 24 rolls.

Yummy Apple Oatmeal

1 apple, any variety, peeled and finely chopped
2⅓ C. apple juice
1⅓ C. quick-cooking rolled oats
1 tsp. ground cinnamon
½ tsp. salt

2 T. raisins
2 tsp. honey
1 tsp. vanilla extract
Vanilla yogurt, optional
Chopped walnuts, optional

In a medium saucepan over medium heat, combine apple, apple juice, oats, cinnamon and salt. Bring mixture to a boil; boil for 1 minute, stirring occasionally. Remove from heat and stir in raisins, honey and vanilla. Cover and let stand for 5 minutes. Serve hot, topped with yogurt and a sprinkling of walnuts, if desired. Makes 4 servings.

Next Day A.M. Bread Pudding

6 eggs
1 C. milk
½ C. heavy cream
1 T. vanilla extract
1 tsp. ground nutmeg
1 (1 lb.) loaf cinnamon-raisin bread, cubed

2 Jonathan apples, peeled and cored
1 C. brown sugar
1 tsp. ground cinnamon
¼ C. butter, melted
1 Jonathan apple
1 T. lemon juice, optional

Grease a 9 x 13" baking dish; set aside. In a large bowl, whisk together eggs, milk, cream, vanilla and nutmeg until well blended. Fold in bread cubes and let stand 5 to 10 minutes to soak. Meanwhile, slice two apples into a medium bowl. Add brown sugar, cinnamon and melted butter; toss well. Arrange apple mixture over bottom of prepared dish. Spoon bread mixture over apples. Cover and refrigerate overnight. When ready to bake, preheat oven to 375°. Peel, core and dice remaining apple; toss with lemon juice, if desired. Arrange apple over bread pudding mixture. Cover and bake for 40 minutes or until bread is no longer soggy. Uncover and set oven to broil. Broil until golden brown on top, about 5 minutes. Remove and let stand 5 to 10 minutes before serving. Makes 12 servings.

Whole Wheat Apple Pancakes

1 C. diced apple, any variety
¾ C. flour
¾ C. whole wheat flour
2 tsp. baking powder
½ tsp. baking soda
¼ tsp. salt

1 C. buttermilk
¾ C. milk
2 eggs
1 T. honey
Maple syrup

Preheat oven to 250°. Place apple in a microwave-safe bowl, cover and microwave on high for about 2 minutes or until softened; set aside. Meanwhile, in a large bowl, mix flour, whole wheat flour, baking powder, baking soda and salt. In a medium bowl, whisk together buttermilk, milk, eggs and honey; gradually add flour mixture to milk mixture, stirring until just combined. Heat a large nonstick griddle or skillet over medium heat until a drop of water pops. For each pancake, spoon about ¼ cup batter onto griddle and sprinkle top with some drained diced apple. Drizzle a little more batter over apples. Cook until tops are bubbly and edges are dry, about 2 minutes. Flip and cook until golden brown, 1 to 2 minutes more. Keep pancakes warm on a baking sheet in oven. Serve warm with syrup. Makes about 12 pancakes.

Overnight Apple French Toast

1 C. brown sugar
½ C. butter
2 T. light corn syrup
2 tart apples, any variety, peeled
3 eggs
1 C. milk

1 tsp. vanilla extract
9 slices day-old French bread (¾" thick)
1 C. applesauce
1 (10 oz.) jar apple jelly
½ tsp. ground cinnamon
⅛ tsp. ground cloves

In a saucepan over medium heat, combine brown sugar, butter and corn syrup. Cook and stir until thickened, 5 to 7 minutes. Pour into an ungreased 9 x 13" baking dish. Core and slice apples ¼" thick; arrange over brown sugar mixture and set aside. In a medium bowl, whisk together eggs, milk and vanilla until well blended. Dip bread into egg mixture and soak for 1 minute; arrange slices over apples. Cover and refrigerate overnight. Before baking, let dish stand at room temperature for 30 minutes. Preheat oven to 350°. Bake uncovered for 35 to 40 minutes or until cooked through. Meanwhile, in a saucepan over medium-low heat, combine applesauce, jelly, cinnamon and cloves; cook until heated through, stirring frequently. Serve applesauce mixture with French toast. Makes 9 servings.

Apple & Sausage Breakfast Bake

1 (12 oz.) day-old baguette
8 eggs
3 C. milk
½ C. sugar, divided
1 T. vanilla extract
¼ tsp. ground nutmeg
¼ tsp. salt
5 to 6 Granny Smith apples

1 T. lemon juice
2 T. maple syrup
2 T. butter, melted
1 tsp. ground cinnamon
1 lb. breakfast sausage, cooked and drained
Powdered sugar

Preheat oven to 375°. Butter a 9 x 13" baking dish. Slice the baguette into 20 (¾" to 1") slices and arrange slices in prepared dish; set aside. In a medium bowl, beat eggs. Whisk in milk, ¼ cup sugar, vanilla, nutmeg and salt until well blended. Pour egg mixture over bread and let soak. Meanwhile, peel and core apples; slice thinly and place in a large bowl. Drizzle with lemon juice, syrup and melted butter; toss to coat. Sprinkle with cinnamon and toss again. Spread cooked sausage over bread. Top with apple mixture. Bake for 30 to 40 minutes or until apples are soft and eggs are set. Cut into squares, sprinkle with powdered sugar and serve warm. Makes 10 servings.

Ham & Apple Casserole

2 C. diced ham
2 C. peeled, cored and chopped apples, any variety
¼ C. raisins
⅓ C. brown sugar
¾ tsp. ground apple pie spice, divided
⅓ C. maple syrup

1 egg
½ C. chopped pecans
⅓ C. powdered sugar
2 T. bourbon
⅛ tsp. cayenne pepper, optional
Warm biscuits, optional

Preheat oven to 350°. Generously grease a 9 x 9˝ baking dish. Arrange ham, apples and raisins in prepared dish and set aside. In a small bowl, mix brown sugar, ½ teaspoon apple pie spice, syrup and egg. Stir in pecans. Spoon mixture over ham and apples. Bake for 35 to 40 minutes or until evenly browned. Meanwhile, in a small bowl, whisk together powdered sugar, bourbon, remaining ¼ teaspoon apple pie spice and cayenne pepper to reach drizzling consistency. Add more milk as needed. Cool casserole for 5 minutes before drizzling glaze over casserole. Serve with biscuits, if desired. Makes 6 servings.

Fruit-Topped Baked Pancake

1½ C. crisp rice cereal
½ C. flour
2 T. plus ⅓ C. sugar
2 eggs
1 C. milk
1 T. vegetable oil
2 T. butter

1 tsp. ground cinnamon
3 C. peeled, thinly sliced tart apples, any variety
½ C. fresh raspberries
½ C. fresh blueberries
1 tsp. powdered sugar

Preheat oven to 425°. In a blender container, combine cereal, flour, 2 tablespoons sugar, eggs, milk and oil; blend for 15 seconds or until smooth. Heat a 10″ pie plate in oven for 5 minutes. Remove plate from oven and spray with nonstick cooking spray. Pour cereal batter into prepared pie plate. Bake about 20 minutes or until golden brown and puffy around edges. Meanwhile, in a large skillet over medium heat, melt butter. Add remaining ⅓ cup sugar, cinnamon, apples and ¼ cup water. Simmer for 10 minutes, stirring occasionally, or until apples are just tender. Remove from heat and stir in raspberries and blueberries. When pancake is done, sprinkle powdered sugar over top and spoon apple mixture over hot pancake. Serve immediately. Makes 4 to 6 servings.

Dutch Baby Apple Pancake

½ C. half & half
3 eggs
½ tsp. vanilla extract
6 T. butter, melted, divided
½ C. flour
¼ tsp. salt
½ tsp. ground cinnamon, divided

3 T. brown sugar
2 T. lemon juice
2 Granny Smith apples, peeled, cored and sliced
¼ C. chopped walnuts, optional
Powdered sugar

Preheat oven to 375°. In a blender container, combine half & half, eggs, vanilla and 2 tablespoons butter; blend until smooth. Add flour, salt and ¼ teaspoon cinnamon; blend and set batter aside. In a 10″ nonstick, oven-proof skillet over medium-high heat, mix remaining ¼ cup butter, remaining ¼ teaspoon cinnamon, brown sugar and lemon juice; bring to a boil while stirring. Stir in apples and reduce heat to low; simmer, stirring often, until apples are tender and liquid has thickened, about 7 minutes. Remove from heat. Pour prepared batter over apple mixture in skillet. Sprinkle with walnuts. Transfer skillet to oven and bake for 25 to 30 minutes or until top is set and golden. Sprinkle with powdered sugar and serve warm. Makes 4 to 6 servings.

Salads & Sides

Updated Waldorf Salad

½ C. heavy cream
1 to 2 T. sugar
¼ C. mayonnaise
Dash of ground nutmeg
2 C. chopped apples, any variety
Juice of 1 lemon

¼ C. chopped celery
¼ C. chopped walnuts or pecans
¼ C. dried sweetened cranberries
  or raisins
½ C. seedless green grapes, halved
½ C. miniature marshmallows, optional

In a small chilled mixing bowl, beat cream on medium speed until frothy. Gradually beat in sugar until soft peaks form. Fold in mayonnaise and nutmeg; set aside. In a large bowl, toss apples with lemon juice. Stir in celery, walnuts, cranberries, grapes and marshmallows, if desired. Add mayonnaise mixture and toss until well coated. Cover and chill before serving. Makes 5 servings.

Variation: Stir in 1 to 2 cups diced cooked turkey or chicken and serve on croissants or whole wheat pita rounds.

Candy Apple Salad

1 egg, beaten
½ C. sugar
1 T. flour
1 T. white vinegar
1 (8 oz.) can crushed pineapple, with juice
1 (8 oz.) container whipped topping, thawed
4 C. peeled, chopped Granny Smith apples
1 C. coarsely chopped dry roasted peanuts, divided

In a medium saucepan over medium heat, stir together egg, sugar, flour, vinegar and pineapple until well combined. Cook until thick, about 6 minutes. Set aside to cool completely. In a large bowl, fold together cooled pineapple mixture and whipped topping. Gently stir in apples and ½ cup peanuts until coated. Sprinkle remaining ½ cup peanuts on top before serving. Makes 8 servings.

Autumn Gelatin Squares

1 (20 oz.) can crushed pineapple, with juice
⅔ C. sugar
1 (3 oz.) pkg. lemon gelatin
1 (8 oz.) pkg. cream cheese, softened

1 C. diced apple, any variety
½ C. chopped pecans or almonds
1 C. chopped celery
1 C. whipped topping
Lettuce leaves, optional

In a medium saucepan, combine pineapple and sugar. Bring mixture to a boil and boil for 3 minutes. Add gelatin and stir until dissolved. Stir in cream cheese until well blended. Let mixture cool. Fold in apple, pecans, celery and whipped topping. Pour mixture into a 9 x 9" pan and chill until firm. Cut and serve on lettuce leaves, if desired. Makes 6 servings.

Red Hot Apple Salad

½ C. red hot candies
1 (6 oz.) pkg. cherry gelatin
2 C. applesauce
1 T. lemon juice
Dash of salt

½ C. chopped almonds or pecans
1 (8 oz.) pkg. cream cheese, softened
¼ C. milk
2 T. mayonnaise

In a large bowl, combine candies and gelatin. Add 3 cups boiling water and stir until dissolved, about 3 minutes. Stir in applesauce, lemon juice and salt to blend. Chill until partially set. Stir in almonds. Pour mixture into an 8 x 8″ pan. Cover and refrigerate until set. In a small mixing bowl, beat together cream cheese, milk and mayonnaise until smooth. Spread over gelatin. Cut to serve. Makes 8 servings.

Homemade Applesauce

4 to 6 assorted cooking apples, peeled, cored and sliced*
2 tsp. lemon juice, optional
1 to 2 T. sugar

1 to 2 T. brown sugar
½ tsp. ground cinnamon
½ tsp. vanilla extract, optional

Place apples in a medium saucepan and add ½ cup water.** Stir in lemon juice, if desired. Place pan over medium heat and bring to a boil; cover and reduce heat to low. Simmer for 15 to 25 minutes or until apples are very soft. Remove from heat and mash apples with a potato masher, fork or wire whisk. Stir in sugar, brown sugar, cinnamon and vanilla, if desired. Return to low heat and cook 5 to 10 minutes more, stirring frequently, to blend flavors and reach desired consistency. Serve warm or chilled. Makes 4 to 6 servings.

Adjust the amount of sugar according to sweetness of apples used.

**You may use unsweetened apple juice or apple cider in place of water. Increase the amount of liquid slightly for thinner applesauce.*

Snickering Apple Salad

1 (12 oz.) container whipped topping, thawed
1 (5 oz.) pkg. vanilla instant pudding mix
6 Red Delicious apples, cored and chopped
6 (2.07 oz.) Snickers candy bars, chopped and chilled
1 banana, peeled and sliced, optional
½ C. caramel ice cream topping
½ C. chopped peanuts

In a large bowl, mix whipped topping and dry pudding mix until well blended. Add apples and candy pieces to pudding mixture and stir well. Fold in banana, if desired. Transfer mixture to a serving bowl. In a microwave-safe bowl, microwave caramel topping until warm enough to drizzle. Drizzle topping over salad and sprinkle peanuts on top. Cover and chill at least 1 hour before serving. Makes 12 servings.

Simple Dutch Apple Salad

2 T. flour
1 T. sugar
1 C. milk
1 egg, lightly beaten
2 Golden Delicious apples

2 Red Delicious apples
½ C. chopped celery
½ C. seedless red grapes, quartered
½ C. chopped walnuts, toasted*

In a small saucepan, mix flour and sugar. Gradually whisk in milk until smooth. Cook over medium-high heat until thickened and bubbly, stirring constantly. Reduce heat to low; cook and stir for 2 minutes longer. Remove from heat. Stir a small amount of hot mixture into egg; then return all to saucepan, stirring constantly. Cook and stir for 2 minutes. Transfer dressing mixture to a bowl and cool to room temperature without stirring. Cover surface of dressing with waxed paper and refrigerate until chilled. Before serving, core and chop all apples. Combine with celery and grapes in a bowl. Drizzle with dressing and toss gently to coat. Sprinkle walnuts over salad. Makes 8 servings.

To toast, place walnuts in a single layer in a dry skillet over medium heat or on a baking sheet in a 350° oven for 8 to 10 minutes or until golden brown.

Sauerkraut-Apple Crunch

1 green or red tart apple, any variety
2 (14 oz.) cans sauerkraut, drained
  and rinsed
¾ C. chopped onion
¾ C. chopped dill pickle
3 T. lemon juice

1 T. sugar
1 T. dried basil
1 T. dill weed
1 T. dried parsley flakes
1 tsp. salt
¼ C. vegetable oil

Peel, core and chop apple; place in a large bowl. Add sauerkraut, onion, pickle, lemon juice, sugar, basil, dill weed, parsley and salt; mix well. Drizzle with oil and toss to coat. Cover and refrigerate at least 2 hours before serving. Makes 8 servings.

Tangy & Tart Apple Salad

4 Granny Smith apples
¼ C. blanched slivered almonds, toasted*

¼ C. dried sweetened cranberries
¼ C. chopped dried cherries
1 C. vanilla yogurt

Core and chop apples; place in a medium bowl. Add almonds, cranberries, cherries and yogurt, stirring until evenly coated. Chill before serving. Makes 4 to 6 servings.

To toast, place almonds in a single layer in a dry skillet over medium heat or on a baking sheet in a 350° oven for 6 to 8 minutes or until golden brown.

Apple-Citrus Salad

¼ C. lime juice
¼ C. lemon juice
¾ C. plus 2 T. orange juice
2 T. apple cider vinegar
1 C. vegetable oil
1¾ tsp. salt
¼ tsp. pepper
¾ tsp. dry mustard

2 cloves garlic, minced
¾ head romaine lettuce
1 bunch arugula
1 Fuji or Gala apple, cored and chopped
1 C. shredded red cabbage
3 green onions, sliced
½ C. diced red or yellow bell pepper
2 medium carrots, shredded

Make dressing at least one day before serving. In a 1-quart jar with tight-fitting lid, combine all juices, vinegar, oil, salt, pepper, dry mustard and garlic. Cover jar and shake well to blend; refrigerate. Wash lettuce and arugula; pat dry. Tear greens and combine in a large bowl. Add apple, cabbage, green onions, bell pepper and carrots; toss well. Shake prepared dressing and serve with salad. Makes 4 to 6 servings.

Apple Coleslaw

1 green or red tart apple, any variety
2 C. shredded green cabbage or coleslaw mix
½ C. chopped celery
½ C. chopped green bell pepper

¼ C. vegetable oil
2 T. lemon juice
2 T. honey
1 tsp. celery seed

Core and chop apple; place in a large bowl. Add cabbage, celery and bell pepper; toss gently and set aside. In a small bowl, whisk together oil, lemon juice, honey and celery seed until blended. Pour dressing mixture over cabbage mixture and toss to coat. Makes 4 servings.

Red Cabbage & Apple Slaw

½ C. plain yogurt
¼ C. sour cream
2 tsp. honey
1 Granny Smith apple, peeled, cored and chopped

2 C. shredded red cabbage
3 T. minced onion
¼ C. chopped fresh parsley
Salt and pepper to taste

In a medium bowl, whisk together yogurt, sour cream and honey. Cover and refrigerate until chilled. Place apple in a medium bowl. Add cabbage, onion and parsley; toss to blend. Season with salt and pepper. Mix again and chill until serving. Makes 4 servings.

Spinach & Apple Salad

2 T. olive oil
1 T. apple cider vinegar
1 tsp. Dijon mustard
Salt and pepper to taste
5 oz. baby spinach leaves (about 5 C. lightly packed)

1 green or red tart apple, any variety, cored
⅓ C. chopped walnuts, toasted*

In a small bowl, whisk together oil, vinegar and Dijon mustard until well blended. Season with salt and pepper. In a large bowl, toss spinach with dressing mixture until evenly coated. Divide spinach among four serving plates. Slice apple into matchsticks and divide evenly over spinach. Top with walnuts and serve promptly. Makes 4 servings.

To toast, place walnuts in a single layer in a dry skillet over medium heat or on a baking sheet in a 350° oven for approximately 10 minutes or until golden brown.

Apple-Cheddar Toss

10 C. torn mixed salad greens
1 red or yellow apple, any variety, cored and chopped
1 C. cubed Cheddar cheese
1 C. chopped walnuts, toasted*
⅔ C. honey
2 T. apple cider vinegar

1 tsp. celery seed
1 tsp. dry mustard
1 tsp. paprika
1 tsp. lemon juice
1 tsp. grated onion
¼ tsp. salt
1 C. vegetable oil

In a large salad bowl, combine greens, apple, cheese and walnuts; toss lightly and set aside. In a blender container or food processor, combine honey, vinegar, celery seed, dry mustard, paprika, lemon juice, onion and salt. While processing, gradually add oil in a steady stream until incorporated. Serve dressing with salad. Makes 10 servings.

To toast, place walnuts in a single layer in a dry skillet over medium heat or on a baking sheet in a 350° oven for approximately 10 minutes or until golden brown.

Broiled Apple & Goat Cheese Salad

2 T. raspberry or red wine vinegar
½ tsp. Dijon mustard
½ tsp. minced garlic
½ tsp. salt
½ tsp. pepper
⅓ C. olive oil

1 T. chopped fresh parsley
3 Belgian endives, cored
1 bunch spinach, rinsed
1 Granny Smith apple, cored
4 oz. mild goat cheese
¼ C. chopped walnuts

In a jar with a tight-fitting lid, combine vinegar, Dijon mustard, garlic, salt and pepper; shake well to blend. Add oil and parsley; shake again. Separate endive leaves and arrange several leaves on each salad plate. Top with spinach leaves and set aside. Quarter and slice apple into 16 wedges. Cut cheese into four thick slices. On broiler pan, arrange four apple slices in a fan shape, sides overlapping, and top with a slice of cheese. Repeat to make three more servings. Broil about 5 minutes or until golden brown on top. Remove apple fans with a spatula and set one on spinach on each plate. Drizzle with salad dressing and sprinkle with walnuts. Makes 4 servings.

Curried Spinach Salad

2 (5 to 6 oz.) pkgs. baby spinach leaves (10 to 12 C. lightly packed)
1 apple, any variety, cored and chopped
¼ C. raisins or dried sweetened cranberries
2 T. chopped peanuts

2 T. olive oil
1 T. sugar
1 T. apple cider vinegar
1 T. mango chutney or apple butter
¾ tsp. curry powder
¼ tsp. salt

In a large bowl, combine spinach, apple, raisins and peanuts. In a jar with a tight-fitting lid, combine oil, sugar, vinegar, chutney, curry powder and salt. Cover jar and shake well to blend. Drizzle dressing mixture over salad and toss to coat. Serve promptly. Makes 6 to 8 servings.

Note: For a main dish salad, add pieces of grilled chicken.

Apple & Rice Salad

1 C. cooked brown rice, chilled
1 C. cooked wild rice, chilled
2 C. chopped apples, any variety
1 C. thinly sliced celery
¼ C. hulled sunflower seeds
¼ C. dried sweetened cranberries
  or currants
2 T. balsamic vinegar

1 T. olive oil
2 tsp. honey
2 tsp. Dijon mustard
2 tsp. orange zest
½ tsp. minced garlic
Salt to taste
Spinach or lettuce leaves, optional

In a large bowl, combine brown rice, wild rice, apples, celery, sunflower seeds and cranberries; stir to combine and set aside. In a container with a tight-fitting lid, combine vinegar, oil, honey, Dijon mustard, orange zest, garlic and salt; cover and shake well. Pour over rice mixture and toss gently to coat. To serve, arrange spinach or lettuce leaves on serving plates, if desired, and divide rice mixture among plates. Serve promptly or cover and chill for up to 4 hours. Makes 6 servings.

Salmon-Apple Salad

2 (4.5 oz.) pkgs. smoked salmon,
  skin removed
1 C. diced Granny Smith apple
1 C. chopped seedless cucumber
¼ C. chopped red onion
2 T. sour cream
2 T. mayonnaise

1 T. apple cider vinegar
1 tsp. Dijon mustard
½ tsp. sugar
⅛ tsp. white pepper
¼ C. heavy cream, whipped
4 C. mixed salad greens

Break salmon into bite-size pieces and place in a medium bowl. Add apple, cucumber and red onion; toss to mix. In a small bowl, stir together sour cream, mayonnaise, vinegar, Dijon mustard, sugar and white pepper. Gently fold in whipped cream until well blended. Pour sour cream mixture over salmon mixture and toss gently to coat. Divide salad greens among four plates and spoon salmon mixture onto greens. Makes 4 servings.

Crabby Apple Slaw

- 1 C. mayonnaise
- ¼ C. lemon juice
- 1½ T. rice vinegar
- 1½ T. sugar
- ¾ tsp. salt
- ¼ tsp. pepper
- 1 tart apple, any variety
- 1 (8 oz.) pkg. imitation crabmeat, flaked
- 1 C. shredded green cabbage
- ⅓ C. thinly sliced red bell pepper
- ⅓ C. shredded carrot

In a large bowl, whisk together mayonnaise, lemon juice, vinegar, sugar, salt and pepper until well blended. Peel, core and dice apple; add to bowl. Stir in crabmeat, cabbage, bell pepper and carrot, tossing to mix well. Divide slaw mixture among four plates and serve promptly. Makes 4 servings.

Tuna Macaroni Salad

1 (16 oz.) pkg. uncooked tri-color pasta
1 C. creamy salad dressing or mayonnaise
½ (1 oz.) env. ranch salad dressing mix
1 (12 oz.) can tuna, drained and flaked
⅓ C. shredded Cheddar cheese

1 apple, any variety, peeled, cored and chopped
1 large carrot, peeled and chopped
⅓ C. raisins

In a large pot of lightly salted boiling water, cook pasta for 8 to 10 minutes or until al dente. Drain and rinse under cold water; drain again. In a large bowl, whisk together salad dressing and ranch dressing mix until blended. Add pasta, tuna, cheese, apple, carrot and raisins; toss to coat. Cover and chill at least 1 hour. Makes 10 servings.

Spicy Ham & Apple Pasta

2 C. uncooked bow tie pasta
2 apples, any variety, cored and
   thinly sliced
2 C. cubed ham
1 C. pineapple preserves
1 C. apple jelly

¼ C. prepared horseradish,
   or less to taste
1½ tsp. dry mustard
1 tsp. pepper
8 oz. mixed salad greens

In a large pot of lightly salted water, cook pasta for 8 to 10 minutes or until al dente. Drain and rinse under cold water; drain again. Transfer pasta to a large bowl; add apples and ham. In a small bowl, whisk together preserves, jelly, horseradish, dry mustard and pepper until blended. Pour over pasta mixture and stir to combine. Cover and refrigerate at least 30 minutes. To serve, divide salad greens among four plates and top with ham salad. Makes 4 servings.

Fall Harvest Bake

1 butternut squash, peeled
2 apples, any variety, cored
½ C. brown sugar
1 T. flour

¼ C. butter, melted
½ tsp. salt
½ tsp. ground mace

Preheat oven to 350°. Cut squash into ¾" slices; quarter and slice apples into wedges. Arrange squash over bottom of a 9 x 13" baking dish. Top with apples and set aside. In a small bowl, mix brown sugar, flour, butter, salt and mace until well blended. Spoon mixture evenly over apples. Bake for 50 to 60 minutes or until tender. Makes 4 servings.

Smashed Sweet Potatoes

2 sweet potatoes, peeled
1 Granny Smith apple, peeled and cored
2 T. butter
¼ C. sugar

1 tsp. ground cinnamon
½ tsp. ground allspice
2 T. milk

Dice sweet potatoes and place in a medium saucepan. Add water to cover and bring to a boil over high heat. Reduce heat and simmer for 20 minutes or until tender. Drain and set aside. Thinly slice apple. In a small saucepan over low heat, melt butter. Stir in sugar, cinnamon and allspice. Add apple, cover and let simmer for 5 to 10 minutes or until apples are tender. Add apple mixture and milk to sweet potatoes. Mash well with a fork, potato masher or electric mixer. Makes 6 servings.

Granny's Baked Bean Casserole

1 C. diced onion
2 (15 oz.) cans Boston-style
   baked beans
1 C. diced Granny Smith apple

1 T. prepared yellow mustard
¼ C. brown sugar
1 tsp. salt
5 bacon strips

Preheat oven to 350°. Grease a 2-quart baking dish; set aside. In a large bowl, stir together onion, beans, apple, mustard, brown sugar and salt until well mixed. Pour mixture into prepared dish. Arrange uncooked bacon strips over the top. Cover and bake about 45 minutes or until thick and bubbly. Uncover and bake 5 minutes longer. Makes 8 servings.

Baked Apple-Carrot Combo

6 large carrots, peeled
4 apples, any variety, peeled and cored
5 T. flour
1 T. brown sugar

½ tsp. ground nutmeg
½ tsp. salt
1 T. butter, cut into small pieces
½ C. orange juice

Preheat oven to 350°. Lightly grease a 2-quart casserole dish; set aside. Slice carrots; quarter and slice apples. In a large saucepan of boiling water, parcook carrots for 5 minutes; drain. Layer carrots and apples in prepared dish; set aside. In a small bowl, mix flour, brown sugar, nutmeg and salt. Sprinkle mixture over carrots and apples. Dot with butter. Pour orange juice over flour mixture. Bake for 30 minutes or until carrots are tender. Makes 6 servings.

Stir-Fry Wild Rice

2 T. olive oil
2 T. finely minced onion
1 T. curry powder
1 apple, any variety, peeled

1 C. chopped mushrooms
¼ C. dried cherries
1½ C. cooked wild rice
Salt and pepper to taste

In a small skillet over medium-high heat, heat oil. Add onion and curry powder; sauté until onion is tender, stirring frequently. Core and dice apple; add to skillet with mushrooms and cherries. Cook and stir until mushrooms are heated through. Add wild rice and stir-fry until hot and tender. Season with salt and pepper. Makes 4 servings.

Cornbread Stuffing

2 (8.5 oz.) pkgs. corn muffin mix
Egg and milk as directed on
   muffin package
1 lb. pork sausage links, thinly sliced
½ lb. fresh mushrooms, sliced
1 C. chopped celery
1 C. chopped onion
1 tsp. chopped garlic
1 Granny Smith apple
8 slices white bread, cubed
Salt and pepper to taste

Prepare batter with corn muffin mix, egg and milk according to package directions and bake as cornbread in two 8 x 8˝ baking pans as directed. Cool cornbread completely and then crumble. Preheat oven to 350°. In a large skillet over medium-high heat, cook sausage until evenly browned. Drain and set aside. In the same skillet over medium heat, sauté mushrooms, celery, onion and garlic until tender; set aside. Peel, core and chop apple and place in a large bowl. Add crumbled cornbread, sausage, mushroom mixture, cubed bread, salt and pepper; mix gently. Transfer mixture to a large casserole dish and bake for 45 minutes or until lightly browned. Makes 9 servings.

Thanksgiving Stuffing

1½ C. cubed whole wheat bread
3¾ C. cubed white bread
1 lb. ground turkey or pork sausage
1 C. chopped onion
¾ C. chopped celery
2½ tsp. dried sage
1½ tsp. dried rosemary

½ tsp. dried thyme
1 Golden Delicious apple, cored and chopped
¾ C. dried sweetened cranberries
⅓ C. minced fresh parsley
¾ C. turkey stock or broth
¼ C. butter, melted

Preheat oven to 350°. On a large jellyroll pan, spread all bread cubes in a single layer. Bake for 5 to 7 minutes or until evenly toasted. Transfer toasted cubes to a large bowl and set aside. In a large skillet over medium heat, combine sausage and onion; cook and stir until meat is evenly browned and crumbly. Add celery, sage, rosemary and thyme; cook and stir for 2 minutes. Pour sausage mixture over toasted bread cubes. Add apple, cranberries and parsley. Drizzle with stock and melted butter; toss lightly to combine. Spread in a large casserole dish and bake for 1 hour. Makes 10 to 12 servings.

Main Dishes

Grilled Turkey-Apple Burgers

1 C. finely chopped peeled apple, any variety
¼ C. finely chopped green onions
1 tsp. ground poultry seasoning
½ tsp. salt
2 T. apple juice or water
1 lb. ground turkey or chicken
4 tsp. honey mustard
4 whole wheat burger buns, split
4 lettuce leaves, optional

Lightly oil the grate and preheat a gas or charcoal grill to medium heat. Meanwhile, in a medium bowl, mix apple, green onions, poultry seasoning, salt and apple juice. Add ground turkey and mix well. Shape meat mixture into four even patties, about ½" thick. Place patties on grate and cover grill. Cook for 14 to 20 minutes or until a meat thermometer inserted in center of patty reaches 165°, flipping patties once partway through cooking time. To serve, spread honey mustard on bottom halves of buns; top with lettuce leaf, turkey patty and top of bun. Makes 4 sandwiches.

Ham & Cheese Panini

2 T. butter
2 Granny Smith apples, peeled, cored and thinly sliced
1 T. chopped fresh thyme

8 slices country-style bread
½ C. whole-grain mustard, or to taste
2 C. shredded Gruyère cheese
8 oz. deli-sliced Black Forest ham

In a large skillet over medium heat, melt butter. Add apples and thyme; cook, stirring occasionally, until apples are softened, about 4 minutes. Cool for 5 minutes. Preheat panini press.* Spread each bread slice with some mustard. Arrange ¼ cup cheese on each of four bread slices. Divide ham evenly among cheese-topped bread and top with an even portion of apple mixture. Follow with remaining cheese and cover with remaining four bread slices. Grill in the panini press until cheese is melted and tops are golden brown and crisp, 5 to 6 minutes. Makes 4 sandwiches.

If a panini press is not available, use a skillet or griddle to toast sandwiches on both sides. Flatten them during cooking, if desired, with a grill press, bacon press or clean foil-wrapped brick.

Chicken Salad Sandwiches

1½ C. cubed cooked chicken
   or turkey breast
1 apple, any variety, cored and chopped
¼ C. diced celery
3 T. mayonnaise
2 T. plain yogurt

2 T. chopped walnuts
2 T. raisins
⅛ tsp. ground nutmeg
⅛ tsp. ground cinnamon
8 slices raisin bread, toasted
4 lettuce leaves

In a medium bowl, mix chicken, apple, celery, mayonnaise, yogurt, walnuts, raisins, nutmeg and cinnamon until well blended. Cover and refrigerate for at least 1 hour. To serve, divide mixture evenly among four slices of toasted bread; top with a lettuce leaf and remaining bread. Makes 4 sandwiches.

Creamy Squash & Apple Soup

1 (1½ to 2 lb.) acorn or butternut squash
2 Haralson or other tart cooking apples
2 T. butter
1 onion, sliced
1 tsp. dried thyme
¼ tsp. dried basil

2 (14 oz.) cans chicken broth
½ C. half & half
1 tsp. ground nutmeg
½ tsp. salt
¼ tsp. white pepper

Cut squash in half; remove seeds and fibers. Cook until tender in oven or microwave and let cool. Remove pulp and set aside; discard rind. Peel, core and slice apples; set aside. In a large saucepan over medium heat, melt butter. Add onion and sauté until crisp-tender, 2 to 3 minutes. Stir in apples, thyme and basil. Cook 2 minutes longer, stirring constantly. Stir in broth. Bring to a boil, then reduce heat and simmer uncovered for 30 minutes. With slotted spoon, remove 1 cup apples; reserve. Working in small batches, use a blender or food processor to puree broth mixture and transfer each batch to a large bowl. Return all pureed soup to saucepan over low heat and add reserved apples. Stir in half & half, nutmeg, salt and white pepper. Cook until hot. Makes 6 servings.

Baked Kielbasa-Apple Rigatoni

1 (16 oz.) pkg. uncooked rigatoni
2 T. olive oil
1 onion, sliced
¼ C. flour
4 C. milk
3 C. shredded Cheddar cheese

1 tsp. hot pepper sauce
1 tsp. salt
1 (14 oz.) pkg. fully-cooked kielbasa, sliced ¼" thick
3 Fuji apples, cored and cubed
2 green onions, thinly sliced

Preheat oven to 350°. Grease a 2½-quart baking dish; set aside. In a large pot of lightly salted boiling water, cook rigatoni until al dente. Drain and return to pot. In a large saucepan over medium heat, heat oil. Add onion and sauté until softened. Stir in flour and cook for 1 minute. Gradually whisk in milk. Bring to a boil, stirring constantly, and cook 1 minute or until thickened; remove from heat. Reserve 1 cup cheese for topping. Stir remaining 2 cups cheese, hot pepper sauce and salt into milk mixture until smooth. To pasta, add kielbasa, apples and cheese sauce; toss well. Spoon into prepared dish, cover and bake for 30 minutes. Uncover, stir and sprinkle top with reserved cheese and green onions. Bake 10 minutes longer. Let stand 10 minutes before serving. Makes 8 servings.

Chicken & Fruit Penne

1 lb. boneless skinless chicken breast strips
4 green onions, sliced
2 tart cooking apples, any variety, cored and thinly sliced
Pinch of ground nutmeg
¾ tsp. salt
¼ tsp. pepper

2 T. apple cider vinegar
1 (12 oz.) can evaporated milk
½ C. dried sweetened cranberries
12 oz. uncooked whole wheat penne
Chopped fresh chives
¼ C. grated Cheddar cheese

Grease a large skillet and place over medium heat. Brown chicken strips on both sides. Transfer chicken to a bowl and set aside. Grease skillet again and add green onions, apples, nutmeg, salt and pepper; sauté for 3 minutes or until softened. Stir in vinegar. Add evaporated milk and cranberries; bring mixture to a boil. Reduce heat and simmer for 3 minutes or until slightly thickened, stirring often. In a large pot of lightly salted water, cook penne to desired doneness. Drain and return to pot. To sauce mixture in skillet, add chicken and any accumulated juices; cook and stir about 3 minutes or until chicken is cooked through. Pour sauce over pasta and toss to coat. Sprinkle with chives and cheese. Makes 8 servings.

Honey-Mustard Chicken

8 pieces bone-in chicken
Salt and pepper to taste
2 T. olive oil
2 Cortland or other baking apples
1 onion, cut into chunks

1 C. chicken broth
2 to 3 T. honey mustard
1½ tsp. butter, softened
1 T. flour

Preheat oven to 450°. Season chicken with salt and pepper. In a large oven-proof skillet over medium-high heat, heat oil. Brown chicken on both sides, 8 to 10 minutes, and transfer to a plate. Pour off all but 2 tablespoons of drippings. Core apples and cut into chunks; add apples and onion to same skillet and cook until slightly softened, about 4 minutes. In a small bowl, whisk together broth and honey mustard; add to skillet and bring to a boil. Return chicken to skillet, skin side up. Transfer skillet to oven and roast uncovered for 15 to 20 minutes or until chicken is cooked through. In a small bowl, mix butter and flour into a paste. Remove chicken, apples and onion to a plate. Place skillet over medium heat to simmer juices. Whisk in half the butter mixture and boil to thicken; whisk in more as needed. Season with salt and pepper. Pour gravy over chicken. Makes 4 servings.

Slow-Cooker Short Ribs

2 apples, any variety, peeled
4 large carrots, peeled
1 onion, cut into wedges
3½ lbs. bone-in beef short ribs
1 C. applesauce
¼ C. apple cider vinegar
2 tsp. minced garlic

1 T. Worcestershire sauce
2 tsp. paprika
1 tsp. dry mustard
1 tsp. salt
1 T. cornstarch
¼ C. apple cider

Core and quarter apples; cut carrots into 1" pieces. In a large slow cooker, arrange apples, carrots and onion. Place short ribs on top; set aside. In a small bowl, combine applesauce, vinegar, garlic, Worcestershire sauce, paprika, dry mustard and salt; mix well. Pour mixture over ribs. Cover and cook on low for 8 to 10 hours or until beef is tender. Transfer beef, apples and vegetables to a serving platter; tent with foil to keep warm. Pour juices from slow cooker into a small saucepan and simmer over medium-low heat for 5 minutes. Meanwhile, mix cornstarch and apple cider until smooth. Pour into simmering juices and bring mixture to a boil. Cook for 1 minute or until sauce thickens. Pour sauce over ribs to serve. Makes 4 servings.

Pork Chop Stuffing Bake

6 boneless pork loin chops (¾" thick)
Salt and pepper to taste
1 T. vegetable oil
¾ C. chopped onion
1 C. chopped celery
2 Granny Smith apples, peeled and coarsely chopped

1 (14.5 oz.) can chicken broth
1 (10.7 oz.) can cream of celery soup
¼ C. dry white wine
6 C. herb-seasoned stuffing cubes

Preheat oven to 375°. Grease a 9 x 13" baking dish; set aside. Season both sides of pork chops with salt and pepper. In a large deep skillet over medium-high heat, heat oil. Brown chops on both sides, turning once. Remove chops from skillet and set aside. To same skillet, add onion and celery; sauté until onion is tender, about 3 minutes. Add apples; cook and stir for 1 minute. Stir in broth, soup and wine; mix well. Bring mixture to a simmer and remove from heat. Stir in stuffing cubes until moistened. Spread mixture in prepared dish and arrange pork chops on top. Pour any accumulated juices over chops. Cover and bake for 30 to 40 minutes or until chops are fully cooked, yet juicy in the center. Makes 6 servings.

Pork Tenderloin with Spicy Salsa

1 (1½ to 2 lb.) pork tenderloin
1 tsp. chili powder
½ tsp. ground cumin
1½ tsp. salt, divided
2 T. olive oil, divided
2 C. diced Fuji or Granny Smith apples
¾ C. chopped red onion
1 tsp. minced garlic

2 T. apple cider vinegar
½ C. chicken broth
1 (4.5 oz.) can chopped green chiles
1 jalapeño pepper, seeded and chopped
1 T. sugar
¼ tsp. pepper
⅓ C. chopped fresh cilantro
¼ tsp. red pepper flakes, optional

Preheat oven to 400°. Rub pork with chili powder, cumin and 1¼ teaspoons salt. In a skillet over medium-high heat, heat 1 tablespoon oil. Brown pork on all sides and transfer to a roasting pan. Heat remaining 1 tablespoon oil in same skillet over medium heat. Cook apples, onion, garlic and vinegar for 5 to 8 minutes. Stir in broth, chiles, jalapeño, sugar, pepper, cilantro and remaining ¼ teaspoon salt. Reduce heat and cook until apples are tender, 20 to 30 minutes, stirring frequently. Stir in red pepper flakes. Meanwhile, roast pork in oven, uncovered, for 20 to 25 minutes or until a meat thermometer reaches 145°. Let stand 5 minutes before slicing. Serve with salsa. Makes 4 to 6 servings.

Grilled Chicken & Apples

6 T. plus ¾ C. apple juice, divided
6 T. lemon juice
1½ T. apple cider vinegar
1½ T. vegetable oil
2 tsp. dried thyme, divided

4 boneless skinless chicken breast halves
2 tart apples, any variety
1 T. honey
2 tsp. cornstarch

In a bowl, mix 6 tablespoons apple juice, lemon juice, vinegar, oil and 1½ teaspoons thyme. Pour half the marinade into a large resealable plastic bag. Add chicken, seal bag and turn several times to coat; refrigerate 2 hours. Refrigerate remaining marinade for later use. To cook, drain and discard marinade from chicken. Peel, core and quarter apples. Dip apples in reserved marinade; set aside. Stir honey into remaining marinade in bowl. Oil the grate and preheat grill to medium heat. Place chicken on grate and cover grill; cook for 4 to 6 minutes on each side, basting frequently with honey marinade. Grill apples for 3 to 5 minutes; baste and turn often until lightly browned. In a saucepan over medium heat, mix remaining ¾ cup apple juice, cornstarch and ½ teaspoon thyme. Boil and whisk for 2 minutes to thicken. Slice grilled apples and add to sauce; serve with grilled chicken. Makes 4 servings.

Grilled Shrimp & Apple Skewers

3 T. honey
3 T. olive oil
1 T. chopped fresh basil
1 T. strawberry jam
¼ tsp. red pepper flakes
½ tsp. minced garlic

2 T. red wine vinegar
1 T. lemon juice
2 tsp. sugar
2 Gala apples, cored
16 jumbo shrimp, peeled and deveined

In a small bowl, whisk together honey, oil, basil, jam, red pepper flakes, garlic, vinegar, lemon juice and sugar until well mixed. Slice each apple into eight wedges and place in a large resealable plastic bag. Add shrimp to bag. Pour honey mixture over apples and shrimp; seal bag and turn several times to coat. Refrigerate to marinate for 30 minutes. To cook, lightly oil the grate and preheat grill to medium-high heat. Thread shrimp and apples alternately on four metal or soaked wooden skewers; discard remaining marinade. Place skewers on grate and cook about 5 minutes per side or until shrimp are opaque. Makes 4 servings.

Desserts & Sweet Things

Apple Squares

1 C. flour
1 tsp. baking powder
¼ tsp. salt
2¼ tsp. ground cinnamon, divided
¼ C. butter, melted
½ C. plus 2 T. sugar, divided

½ C. brown sugar
1 egg
1 tsp. vanilla extract
½ C. chopped apple, any variety
½ C. chopped pecans

Preheat oven to 350°. Grease a 9 x 9″ baking pan; set aside. In a medium bowl, sift together flour, baking powder, salt and ¼ teaspoon cinnamon; set aside. In a large bowl, stir together butter, ½ cup sugar and brown sugar. Add egg and vanilla, stirring until well blended. Add flour mixture and stir until just combined. Stir in apple and pecans. Spread batter evenly in prepared pan. In a small bowl, mix remaining 2 tablespoons sugar and 2 teaspoons cinnamon; sprinkle over batter. Bake for 25 to 30 minutes or until bars spring back when lightly touched. Cool in pan; cut into squares. Makes 16 servings.

Easy Apple Strudel

⅓ C. sugar
1 tsp. ground cinnamon
2¾ C. peeled, thinly sliced apples, any variety
2 slices day-old bread, crumbled
¼ C. golden raisins or chopped pecans

5 sheets phyllo dough
⅓ C. butter, melted
3 T. milk
1 tsp. vanilla extract
2 C. powdered sugar

Preheat oven to 400°. Line a baking sheet with parchment paper; set aside. In a bowl, mix sugar and cinnamon. In another bowl, mix apples, bread, raisins and most of sugar mixture; set aside. Unfold phyllo dough and cover with a damp towel. Transfer one sheet of phyllo to a clean tea towel; brush butter lightly over entire sheet. Layer a second sheet over butter, edges even. Brush with more butter. Make three more layers of phyllo and butter. Spread apple mixture down length of nearest third of pastry, leaving edges uncovered. Roll pastry over apple filling to form a log. Transfer log to prepared baking sheet, seam side down; seal ends. Brush with butter and sprinkle with remaining sugar mixture. Bake for 30 minutes, until golden brown. Mix milk, vanilla and powdered sugar; drizzle over cooled strudel. Makes 6 servings.

Banana-Apple Cupcakes

2 C. flour
1 tsp. baking soda
1 tsp. salt
½ tsp. ground cinnamon
½ tsp. ground nutmeg
⅓ C. vegetable shortening
1¼ C. sugar
⅓ C. unsweetened applesauce

2 eggs
1 tsp. vanilla extract
¼ C. buttermilk
1 C. mashed ripe bananas
1⅓ C. peeled, finely chopped apples, any variety
1 (16 oz.) can cream cheese frosting

Preheat oven to 350°. Line 24 muffin cups with paper liners; set aside. In a medium bowl, sift together flour, baking soda, salt, cinnamon and nutmeg; set aside. In a large mixing bowl, cream shortening and sugar. Beat in applesauce and eggs. Stir in vanilla and buttermilk. Beat in flour mixture until just blended. Fold in bananas and apples. Divide batter among prepared muffin cups, filling each cup about ½ full. Bake for 20 to 25 minutes or until a toothpick inserted near center comes out clean. Let cool before spreading frosting on top. Makes 24 cupcakes.

Spiced Apple Cookies

¼ C. vegetable shortening
¼ C. plus 1 T. butter, softened, divided
1⅓ C. brown sugar
1 egg
2 C. flour
1 tsp. baking soda
½ tsp. salt
1 tsp. ground cinnamon

½ tsp. ground cloves
¼ tsp. ground nutmeg
1 C. chopped walnuts
1 C. peeled, grated apple, any variety
1 C. raisins
¼ C. milk, plus extra for icing
1½ C. powdered sugar
1 tsp. clear vanilla extract

Preheat oven to 375°. Line baking sheets with parchment paper; set aside. In a large mixing bowl, beat shortening, ¼ cup butter and brown sugar until fluffy. Beat in egg. In a separate bowl, mix flour, baking soda, salt, cinnamon, cloves and nutmeg. Stir in half the flour mixture. Add walnuts, apple and raisins. Stir in remaining flour mixture and ¼ cup milk. Drop by tablespoonfuls onto prepared baking sheets and bake for 9 to 12 minutes. Cool on wire racks. For icing, whisk together powdered sugar, remaining 1 tablespoon butter, vanilla and enough milk to reach desired consistency. Spread on cookies. Makes 36 cookies.

Apple Ice Cream

1 C. sugar, divided
1 C. milk
¼ tsp. salt
3 egg yolks, beaten
2 C. heavy cream
1 tsp. vanilla extract

Food coloring, optional
3 apples, any variety, peeled, cored and diced
1 T. lemon juice
Caramel ice cream topping, optional

In a small saucepan over medium heat, combine ½ cup sugar, milk, salt and egg yolks. Bring mixture just to a boil, stirring constantly, and then promptly remove from heat. Let cool slightly; transfer mixture to a chilled bowl and refrigerate for 1 to 1½ hours or until mixture is at room temperature. Stir in cream, vanilla and food coloring, if desired; set aside. In a blender container or food processor, combine half the apples, remaining ½ cup sugar and lemon juice; cover and process by pulsing until coarsely chopped. Add remaining apples, cover and process until finely chopped but not pureed. Stir apple mixture into milk mixture. Pour into a 2-quart ice cream freezer and freeze according to manufacturer's directions. Serve with caramel topping, if desired. Makes 12 servings.

Southern Apple Dumplings

1 (8 oz.) tube refrigerated crescent roll dough
1 large Granny Smith or Gala apple, peeled and cored
½ C. butter
½ C. sugar
¼ C. brown sugar
½ tsp. ground cinnamon
1 tsp. vanilla extract
½ (12 oz.) can lemon-lime or Mountain Dew soda
Vanilla or cinnamon ice cream, optional

Preheat oven to 350°. Grease an 8 x 8˝ baking pan; set aside. Unroll dough and separate into eight triangles. Cut apple into eight even wedges. Place one apple wedge on each dough triangle and starting at the smallest end, roll dough around apple. Pinch to seal and place in prepared dish; set aside. In a small saucepan over low heat, melt butter. Stir in sugar, brown sugar and cinnamon until blended. Remove from heat and stir in vanilla. Pour mixture evenly over apple dumplings. Pour soda into pan around edges. Bake for 35 to 45 minutes or until golden brown. Serve warm with ice cream and drizzle some of the sauce from pan over the top. Makes 8 dumplings.

Apple Turnovers

⅓ C. sugar
¾ tsp. ground cinnamon
1 T. cornstarch
4 tart apples, any variety
1 T. lemon juice

2 T. butter, cubed
Pastry for double-crust pie*
Milk
1 C. powdered sugar
1 tsp. clear vanilla extract

Preheat oven to 400°. Line a baking sheet with parchment paper; set aside. In a small bowl, mix sugar, cinnamon and cornstarch. Peel, core and thinly slice apples into a large bowl; toss with lemon juice. Add butter and sugar mixture; stir to mix. Divide pastry into eight even pieces; on a lightly floured surface, roll each piece into a 5″ square. Spoon filling off-center on each square. Brush edges with milk; fold pastry over filling to form a triangle, edges even. With fork, crimp edges together to seal. Cut slits in top. Place on prepared baking sheet and chill 15 minutes. Brush tops with milk and bake for 35 minutes. In a small bowl, mix powdered sugar, vanilla and enough milk to make a smooth icing; drizzle over slightly cooled turnovers. Makes 8 turnovers.

*Use your favorite pie crust recipe or the recipe on page 91.

One-Crust Blackberry-Apple Pie

1½ C. flour
¾ C. plus 2 T. brown sugar, divided
9 T. butter, softened, divided
3 egg yolks
6 apples, any variety

2½ C. blackberries
1 T. lemon juice
6 T. sugar, divided
Sweetened whipped cream

In a food processor or medium bowl, combine flour, ¾ cup brown sugar, 6 tablespoons butter and egg yolks; mix until smooth dough forms. Shape dough into a ball, wrap in plastic and chill 20 minutes. Meanwhile, peel, core and thinly slice apples. In a large bowl, combine apples and blackberries. Toss with lemon juice and 5 tablespoons sugar. Transfer fruit to a deep 9″ pie plate and set aside. When ready to bake, preheat oven to 425°. On a lightly floured surface, roll dough into a circle large enough to cover top of pie plate. Place dough over fruit filling and flute edges to seal dough against pie plate rim. Sprinkle remaining 1 tablespoon sugar over dough. Bake for 10 minutes. Reduce oven temperature to 375° and bake for 15 to 20 minutes more or until pastry is golden brown. Serve warm with whipped cream. Makes 8 servings.

Rhubarb-Apple Crisp

4 C. sliced rhubarb
4 C. peeled, sliced apples, any variety
1½ C. sugar
7 T. plus ¾ C. flour, divided
½ tsp. salt, divided
1 T. lemon juice

¾ C. brown sugar
½ C. quick-cooking rolled oats
1 tsp. ground cinnamon
¼ tsp. ground nutmeg
½ C. butter, sliced
Whipped topping, optional

Preheat oven to 350°. Generously grease a 9 x 9˝ baking pan; set aside. In a large bowl, combine rhubarb, apples, sugar, 7 tablespoons flour, ¼ teaspoon salt and lemon juice; toss until well mixed. Spoon fruit mixture into prepared pan and set aside. In a medium bowl, mix brown sugar, remaining ¾ cup flour, oats, remaining ¼ teaspoon salt, cinnamon and nutmeg. With a pastry blender or two knives, cut in butter until mixture is crumbly. Sprinkle oats mixture over fruit filling. Bake for 40 to 50 minutes or until topping is golden brown and filling is bubbly. Cool slightly before serving. Garnish with whipped topping, if desired. Makes 9 servings.

Mini Apple Cakes

1 C. brown sugar
⅓ C. molasses
⅓ C. frozen apple juice concentrate, thawed
¾ C. vegetable oil
2 eggs
3 C. flour
2½ tsp. ground apple pie spice
1 tsp. baking powder
1 tsp. baking soda
½ tsp. salt
2½ C. peeled, finely chopped apples, any variety
¾ C. powdered sugar
1 C. heavy cream
1 (8 oz.) pkg. cream cheese, softened
1 tsp. vanilla extract
Ground cinnamon for sprinkling

Preheat oven to 350°. Grease a 9 x 13″ baking pan; line with parchment paper and set aside. In a large mixing bowl, beat brown sugar and molasses until smooth. Add apple juice concentrate, oil and eggs; beat well. In a separate bowl, whisk together flour, apple pie spice, baking powder, baking soda and salt. Add flour mixture and ¾ cup water alternately to molasses mixture, stirring well after each addition. Stir in apples.

continued on next page

Spread batter in prepared pan. Bake for 35 to 40 minutes or until cake springs back when lightly touched in the middle. Remove from oven and let cool about 1 hour. Place cake in freezer for 2 to 3 hours to make cutting easier. To prepare frosting, combine powdered sugar and cream in a small mixing bowl. Beat mixture on high speed until soft peaks form; set aside. In another mixing bowl, use the same beaters to beat cream cheese with vanilla until fluffy. Add about ¼ of the whipped cream and mix on low speed. Fold in remaining whipped cream until well blended; set frosting aside. Trim about ½" from edges of cake; discard. Slice remaining cake into 24 (2") squares. Frost half the cake squares; top with remaining squares and garnish with a dollop of remaining frosting. Sprinkle with cinnamon, if desired. Makes 12 servings.

Apple Pudding Cake with Sauce

1 C. brown sugar
¼ C. plus ⅓ C. butter, softened, divided
1 egg
1 C. flour
1 tsp. baking soda
1½ tsp. ground cinnamon, divided

½ tsp. ground nutmeg
¼ tsp. salt
2 C. chopped apples, any variety
⅔ C. sugar
⅓ C. half & half

Preheat oven to 350°. Grease a 9 x 9" baking pan; set aside. In a large mixing bowl, beat together brown sugar and ¼ cup butter until light and fluffy. Beat in egg. In a separate bowl, whisk together flour, baking soda, 1 teaspoon cinnamon, nutmeg and salt. Add flour mixture to butter mixture and stir until well blended. Stir in apples. Spread batter in prepared pan. Bake for 25 to 35 minutes or until a toothpick inserted near center comes out clean. Meanwhile, in a small saucepan over medium heat, combine remaining ⅓ cup butter, sugar, half & half and remaining ½ teaspoon cinnamon. Cook, stirring frequently, until butter is melted and sauce is heated through. Serve warm sauce over warm cake. Makes 9 servings.

Gingerbread Cobbler

4 C. peeled, sliced apples, any variety
⅓ C. brown sugar
1 T. butter
½ C. original 100% bran cereal
 (not flakes)
¼ C. light molasses
¼ C. vegetable shortening
1 egg, slightly beaten

1 C. flour
¼ C. sugar
1 tsp. baking soda
¼ tsp. salt
¼ tsp. ground cloves
½ tsp. ground ginger
Whipped topping, optional

Preheat oven to 350°. Grease an 8 x 8˝ baking pan. Spread apples over bottom of pan. In a bowl, mix brown sugar and butter until crumbly. Spread over apples and sprinkle with 3 tablespoons water; set aside. In a large bowl, combine cereal, ⅔ cup hot water, molasses and shortening; let stand about 5 minutes. Whisk in egg. In another bowl, stir together flour, sugar, baking soda, salt, cloves and ginger. Add to cereal mixture and stir until combined. Spoon cereal batter over apples. Bake about 40 minutes or until apples are tender. Serve warm or cold with whipped topping, if desired. Makes 12 servings.

Lemon-Kissed Apple Pie Bars

3 C. flour
5 T. plus ¾ C. sugar, divided
½ tsp. salt
1½ tsp. lemon zest
⅔ C. butter
⅔ C. vegetable shortening
2 eggs, separated
¾ to 1 C. milk, plus more for glaze
⅔ C. crushed corn flakes cereal
8 C. peeled, thinly sliced apples, any variety
2 T. lemon juice
1½ C. powdered sugar
1 tsp. vanilla extract

Preheat oven to 350°. In a large bowl, mix flour, 2 tablespoons sugar, salt and lemon zest. With a pastry blender or two knives, cut in butter and shortening until mixture is crumbly. Stir in egg yolks and ½ cup milk until mixture forms a ball, adding more milk as needed, 1 tablespoon at a time. Divide dough into two even balls. On a lightly floured surface, roll out one ball into a 12 x 17" rectangle. Press into bottom and up sides of an ungreased 10 x 15" jellyroll pan. Sprinkle dough evenly with cereal.

continued on next page

Arrange apples over cereal; sprinkle with ¾ cup sugar and drizzle with lemon juice. Roll out remaining dough into a 10 x 15" rectangle. Place over apples and press crust edges together to seal. Lightly beat egg whites and brush over top crust. Sprinkle with remaining 3 tablespoons sugar. Cut slits in top crust. Bake for 55 to 65 minutes or until apples are tender and crust is golden brown. Cool for 1 hour. To make glaze, whisk together powdered sugar, vanilla and enough milk to make a thin icing. Drizzle over bars. Serve warm or cool. Makes 24 servings.

Apple Streusel Cheesecake Bars

1 (1 lb. 1.5 oz.) pkg. oatmeal cookie mix
½ C. butter
2 (8 oz.) pkgs. cream cheese, softened
½ C. plus 2 T. sugar, divided
2 eggs
1 tsp. vanilla extract

3 Granny Smith or Gala apples
½ tsp. ground cinnamon
¼ tsp. ground nutmeg
¼ C. chopped walnuts or pecans
½ C. caramel ice cream topping

Preheat oven to 350°. Line a 9 x 13˝ baking pan with foil and grease lightly; set aside. Pour cookie mix into a large bowl. With a pastry blender or two knives, cut in butter until crumbly. Reserve 1½ cups crumb mixture; press remaining mixture into prepared pan. Bake for 10 minutes. In a large mixing bowl, beat together cream cheese, ½ cup sugar, eggs and vanilla until smooth; spread evenly over partially baked warm crust. Peel, core and finely chop apples into a bowl. Add cinnamon, nutmeg and remaining 2 tablespoons sugar; mix well. Spread apple mixture over cream cheese layer; sprinkle with reserved crumbs and walnuts. Bake for 30 to 40 minutes or until filling is set. Drizzle with caramel topping before serving. Makes 24 servings.

Baked Apple Wedges

3 T. brown sugar, divided
½ C. quick-cooking rolled oats
¼ tsp. ground cinnamon
¼ tsp. ground ginger
Pinch of ground nutmeg
Pinch of ground cloves

¼ C. sliced almonds
4 McIntosh apples
1 egg
1 T. milk
Sweetened whipped cream or
    vanilla ice cream

Preheat oven to 350°. Line a baking sheet with parchment paper and sprinkle 1 tablespoon brown sugar over top; set aside. In a food processor, combine remaining 2 tablespoons brown sugar, oats, cinnamon, ginger, nutmeg and cloves; process until smooth. Add half the almonds and process until finely chopped. Repeat with remaining almonds. Transfer mixture to a shallow bowl. Peel, core and quarter apples. In a small bowl, whisk together egg and milk. Dip apple pieces into egg mixture and let excess drip off. Dip in oatmeal mixture to coat well and place on prepared baking sheet. Bake for 20 to 25 minutes or until soft. Serve warm with whipped cream or ice cream. Makes 8 wedges.

Old-Fashioned Apple Pie

1 (14.1 oz.) pkg. refrigerated pie crust (2 ct.) or homemade pie crust for double-crust 9″ pie*
½ C. sugar
½ C. brown sugar
3 T. flour
1 tsp. ground cinnamon
⅛ tsp. ground nutmeg
¼ tsp. ground ginger, optional
7 C. peeled, thinly sliced pie-baking apples, any variety
1 T. lemon juice
1 T. butter, cut into small pieces
Milk, optional
Coarse sugar, optional

Preheat oven to 375°. Let pie crusts stand at room temperature for 15 minutes. Meanwhile, in a small bowl, stir together sugar, brown sugar, flour, cinnamon, nutmeg and ginger, if desired. In a large bowl, combine apples and lemon juice; toss to coat. Add sugar mixture and mix well. Line a 9″ pie plate with one pie crust; trim crust even with rim of pie plate. Pour apple filling into crust; dot with butter. Place remaining crust

continued on next page

over filling and trim to about ½" beyond edge of pie plate. Fold top crust around edge of bottom crust and pinch edges together to seal. Flute as desired. Cut several slits in top crust and brush with milk and sprinkle lightly with coarse sugar, if desired. Bake for 35 minutes. Then increase oven temperature to 400° and bake 10 to 15 minutes longer or until golden brown. Let cool before cutting. Makes 8 servings.

*Homemade Pie Crust

3 C. flour
1 tsp. salt
1¼ C. vegetable shortening

1 egg, lightly beaten
1 T. white vinegar

In a medium bowl, stir together flour and salt. With a pastry blender or two knives, cut in shortening until mixture is crumbly. In a separate bowl, mix 4 tablespoons cold water, egg and vinegar. Drizzle water mixture over flour mixture and stir until dough holds together. Divide into two flattened balls. On a lightly floured surface, roll each ball into a 12" circle (or to size and shape needed). Makes 2 crusts.

Sour Cream Dutch Apple Pie

2 eggs
1 C. sour cream
1 C. sugar
2 T. plus ¼ C. flour, divided
1 tsp. vanilla extract
¼ tsp. salt

3 C. peeled, chopped tart apples, any variety
1 (9˝) ready-to-bake pie shell
¼ C. brown sugar
3 T. butter

Preheat oven to 375°. In a large bowl, beat eggs. Whisk in sour cream until well blended. Add sugar, 2 tablespoons flour, vanilla and salt; mix well. Stir in apples. Spread mixture in unbaked pie shell and bake for 15 minutes. Meanwhile, in a small bowl, combine brown sugar and remaining ¼ cup flour. With a pastry blender or two knives, cut in butter until mixture is crumbly. Sprinkle over top of pie. Bake for 20 to 25 minutes more or until filling is set and apples are tender. Cool completely before slicing. Makes 8 servings.

Caramel Apple Refrigerator Dessert

2 C. finely crushed vanilla wafers
⅓ C. butter, melted
1 (8 oz.) pkg. cream cheese, softened
¼ C. sugar
3¼ C. milk, divided
1 (8 oz.) container whipped topping, thawed, divided
2 (3.4 oz.) pkgs. vanilla instant pudding mix
½ C. caramel ice cream topping, divided
1 red apple, any variety
1 green apple, any variety
¼ C. peanuts, chopped

In a bowl, mix wafer crumbs and butter. Press mixture into a 9 x 13" baking pan; set aside. In a medium mixing bowl, beat cream cheese, sugar and ¼ cup milk until well blended. Stir in 1 cup whipped topping. Spread cream cheese mixture over crust and set aside. In a large bowl, whisk together remaining 3 cups milk and pudding mixes until beginning to thicken, about 2 minutes. Stir in ¼ cup caramel topping. Spread pudding mixture over cream cheese layer. Top with remaining whipped topping. Cover and chill for 5 hours or until firm. Just before serving, core and chop both apples; sprinkle over dessert and top with peanuts. Drizzle with remaining ¼ cup caramel topping. Makes 16 servings.

Apple Cobbler

- 4 C. peeled, thinly sliced apples, any variety
- 1 C. sugar, divided
- 3 T. lemon juice
- ½ C. apple juice or water
- 1 C. flour
- 2 tsp. baking powder
- ¼ tsp. salt
- ¼ tsp. ground nutmeg
- ½ tsp. ground cinnamon
- ¼ C. butter, softened
- ½ C. milk
- Whipped topping or vanilla ice cream, optional

Preheat oven to 350°. Lightly grease an 8 x 8″ baking pan; set aside. In a large bowl, combine apples and ½ cup sugar. Add lemon juice and apple juice; stir to mix. Pour apple mixture into prepared dish and set aside. In a small bowl, whisk together flour, baking powder, salt, nutmeg and cinnamon; set aside. In a small mixing bowl, combine butter and remaining ½ cup sugar; beat until smooth and creamy. Add milk and mix well. Add flour mixture and mix until blended. Spread batter over apple mixture in dish. Bake for 40 minutes or until crust is golden brown and filling is bubbly. Cool slightly before serving with whipped topping or ice cream. Makes 8 servings.

Gourmet Chocolate-Caramel Apples

5 apples, any variety, stems removed
5 wooden popsicle sticks or skewers
1 (11 oz.) pkg. caramel bits

1 (12 oz.) pkg. milk chocolate chips
Assorted chopped nuts, candy sprinkles or small candies

Wash and dry apples;* remove stems. Push a stick halfway into stem end of each apple. Line a baking sheet with parchment paper and grease lightly; set aside. Fill the bottom of a double boiler halfway with water and bring to a boil over medium-high heat. Place caramel bits and 1 to 2 tablespoons water in top of double boiler and set over boiling water. Heat until melted, stirring frequently. Dip each apple into caramel, turning to coat evenly; let excess caramel drip back into pan. Scrape excess off bottom and set on prepared baking sheet. Refrigerate for 1 hour. In a microwave-safe bowl, microwave chocolate chips on high for 60 seconds to melt; stir and repeat in 15 to 30 second intervals until smooth. Drizzle chocolate over apples. After several minutes, sprinkle with nuts. Let stand at room temperature for 3 hours or until set. Makes 5 apples.

*To remove wax coating, boil 6 cups water and ¼ teaspoon vinegar in a saucepan; dip apples for 4 seconds. Dry thoroughly.

Baked Stuffed Apples

⅓ C. chopped walnuts
⅓ C. chopped pecans
¼ C. brown sugar
¼ tsp. salt
¼ tsp. ground cinnamon
¼ tsp. ground cardamom

¼ C. quick-cooking rolled oats
¼ C. butter, cubed
2 T. raisins
6 Jazz apples or other firm baking variety
1½ C. apple cider
Vanilla ice cream, optional

Preheat oven to 350°. In a bowl, mix walnuts, pecans, brown sugar, salt, cinnamon, cardamom and oats. With a pastry blender or two knives, cut in butter until mixture is crumbly. Stir in raisins and set filling aside. Peel skin off the top third of each apple. With a melon baller or knife, scoop out stem and enough of the core to leave a shell with ½˝-thick walls. Do not cut through bottom of apples. Widen holes at the top. Stuff apples with filling, mounding extra on top. Place filled apples in a 2-quart baking dish. Pour cider around apples and cover with foil. Bake for 45 minutes. Remove foil and bake uncovered for 30 to 45 minutes more or until tender, basting with juices every 15 minutes. Drizzle apples with remaining sauce from pan and serve with ice cream, if desired. Makes 6 apples.

Beverages & Miscellaneous

Fizzy Orchard Punch

1 (32 oz.) bottle apple juice, chilled
1 (12 oz.) can frozen cranberry juice concentrate
1 C. orange juice
1½ L ginger ale
1 apple, any variety

In a large punch bowl or 5-quart bucket, combine apple juice, cranberry juice concentrate and orange juice. Stir to dissolve. Slowly add ginger ale. Slice apple crosswise into thin rings and float them on top of punch. Makes 12 servings.

Homemade Soft Cider

12 assorted sweet and tart apples,
   any variety*
1 orange
½ to 1 C. brown or white sugar
1 whole nutmeg

1 T. whole cloves
4 cinnamon sticks, plus more
   for garnishing
1 tsp. whole allspice, optional

Wash and quarter apples and orange; place in a large pot. Add enough water to cover fruit by at least 2". Stir in ½ cup brown sugar. Add nutmeg, cloves, 4 cinnamon sticks and allspice, if desired. Boil uncovered over medium-high heat for 1 hour, stirring occasionally. Cover and reduce heat to low; simmer about 2 hours longer. Periodically mash fruit as it softens. Add more sugar to taste. Remove from heat and let cool. Strain juice into a large pitcher; discard solids. For naturally cloudy cider, use a colander or metal sieve for straining. For filtered cider, line colander with several layers of cheesecloth or a paper coffee filter and allow juice to drip through slowly (it may take an hour). Serve chilled or hot. Garnish with fresh cinnamon sticks, if desired. Makes about 16 servings.

Try Gala, Granny Smith, Winesap, Braeburn, Jonagold, Grimes Golden or Baldwin apples.

Yogurt-Apple Smoothie

1 apple, any variety, peeled and cored
1 kiwifruit, peeled
4 fresh strawberries

⅔ C. strawberry yogurt
⅓ C. apple juice

Cut apple and kiwifruit into small chunks. In a blender container, combine apple, kiwifruit, strawberries, yogurt and apple juice. Cover and process on high speed for 30 seconds or until smooth. Pour into glasses and serve promptly. Makes 2 servings.

Apple Shake

1 apple, any variety, peeled and cored
1½ C. milk
3 scoops vanilla ice cream or ice milk

2 T. sugar
Dash of ground cinnamon, optional

Chop apple and place in a blender container. Add milk, ice cream and sugar. Blend on high speed until smooth. Pour into glasses and sprinkle with cinnamon, if desired. Serve promptly. Makes 2 servings.

Tropical Punch

1 apple, any variety, peeled and cored
2 qts. orange drink
1 qt. peach or pear nectar
¼ C. lime juice
2 C. small melon cubes (cantaloupe, honeydew or watermelon)
½ C. grenadine syrup, optional
Lime and orange slices, optional
Ice cubes

Chop apple and place in a punch bowl. Add orange drink, nectar, lime juice, melon cubes and grenadine, if desired; stir to blend. Garnish punch with lime and orange slices, if desired. Add ice cubes just before serving. Makes 16 servings.

Iced Apple Sweet Tea

6 individual sweet apple tea bags
1 vanilla bean
1 C. sugar
1 small apple, any variety, cored
   and thinly sliced

½ lemon, thinly sliced
Ice

In a medium saucepan over high heat, boil 6 cups water. Remove from heat and add tea bags. Cover and let cool to room temperature, about 1 hour. Remove and discard tea bags. Meanwhile, to make vanilla syrup, cut vanilla bean in half lengthwise and remove seeds. Place seeds and pod halves in a small saucepan; add sugar and 1 cup water. Bring mixture to a boil over medium heat. Reduce heat and simmer for 5 minutes, stirring occasionally, until sugar is dissolved. Allow syrup to cool for 20 minutes. To mix sweet tea, pour prepared tea into a pitcher and stir in strained vanilla syrup. Add apple and lemon slices. Refrigerate about 1 hour. Serve tea over ice. Makes 6 servings.

Spiced Apple Rings

½ to ¾ C. sugar
⅓ C. red hot candies

1 tsp. red food coloring
4 Winesap apples

In a large saucepan over medium-high heat, combine 1 cup water, sugar, candies and food coloring. Bring mixture to a boil. Reduce heat to medium-low and simmer syrup for 5 minutes, stirring occasionally, until candies have dissolved. Meanwhile, peel and core apples; slice crosswise into rings, ⅜" to ½" thick. Add apple rings to syrup mixture and simmer about 10 minutes or until apples are tender. Stir gently several times during cooking. Remove from heat, cover pan and let apples stand in syrup until cool. Serve at room temperature or refrigerate in syrup. Makes 4 to 6 servings.

Apple Chutney

15 tart apples, any variety
1 yellow onion, quartered
3" piece of fresh gingerroot, peeled
1 C. white wine vinegar
½ C. sugar

½ C. brown sugar
½ tsp. ground cinnamon
½ tsp. white pepper
½ tsp. ground cardamom
¼ tsp. ground nutmeg

Peel, core and chop apples into a large pot. Place pot over medium-high heat and add onion, gingerroot, vinegar, sugar, brown sugar, cinnamon, white pepper, cardamom and nutmeg. Mix well and bring to a boil. Reduce heat to medium-low and simmer for 30 minutes, stirring frequently, until apples are tender. Add water as needed to keep ingredients moist. Remove and discard onion and gingerroot. Let cool. Store in an airtight container in refrigerator. Makes 40 servings.

Creamy Apple Horseradish Sauce

¼ C. grated tart apple, any variety
½ tsp. lemon juice
¼ C. plain yogurt

¼ C. light mayonnaise
1 tsp. Dijon mustard
1 T. prepared horseradish

In a medium bowl, toss together apple and lemon juice. Add yogurt, mayonnaise, Dijon mustard and horseradish; mix well. Cover and refrigerate. Serve with beef or pork dishes. Makes about ¾ cup.

Easy Apple Jelly

3 lbs. fully ripe tart apples, any variety   3 C. sugar
2 T. lemon juice

Wash apples; remove stems and blossom ends but leave cores, seeds and skins (for added natural pectin). Chop apples into a large saucepan; add 3 cups water and place pan over high heat. Cover and bring to a boil. Reduce heat to medium-low and simmer for 20 to 25 minutes or until apples are very soft. Lightly mash apples. Line a colander with cheesecloth and set over a large bowl. Pour apples into colander and allow juice to drain into bowl without pressing fruit, about 30 minutes. Measure exactly 4 cups apple juice into a large saucepan.* Stir lemon juice and sugar into juice. Bring mixture to a boil over high heat and cook to 220° on a candy or jelly thermometer. Remove from heat and skim off foam. Pour into hot, sterilized jars. Wipe rims and cover with lids and screw bands; process in a hot water bath for 5 minutes. Makes about 4 half-pint jars.

Apple pulp may be pressed through a sieve to remove seeds and skins. Mix with sugar and spices and then cook until thickened to make simple apple butter.

Slow-Cooked Apple Butter

6 lbs. assorted sweet and tart apples, any variety
¼ C. apple cider vinegar
1½ C. sugar
½ C. brown sugar

1½ tsp. ground cinnamon
¼ tsp. ground cloves
½ tsp. ground allspice
¼ tsp. salt, optional

Peel, core and slice apples. Place in a large slow-cooker and add vinegar. Cover and cook on high for 8 hours. Reduce heat to low. Stir in sugar, brown sugar, cinnamon, cloves, allspice and salt, if desired. Cover and continue to cook on low for 9 to 10 hours, stirring occasionally. Use a potato masher or immersion blender to puree apples to desired consistency. If thicker mixture is desired, remove cover and cook on low for several more hours to thicken. Spoon into airtight jars or containers and allow apple butter to cool before refrigerating or freezing. Spread on biscuits, muffins, toast, tortillas or peanut butter sandwiches, stir into cottage cheese or hot oatmeal, or pour warm apple butter over ice cream or cake. Makes 4 to 5 cups.

INDEX

Appetizers & Snacks

Apple-Mango Salsa	10
Battered Apple & Onion Rings	7
Broiled Apple Toast	12
Cheddar-Apple Pie Dip	5
Chicken-Apple Stuffed Tomatoes	6
Creamy Toffee Crunch Dip	4
Dried Cinnamon Apple Chips	13
Gala Egg Rolls	8
Jazzed-Up Deviled Eggs	9
Peanut Butter-Bacon Applewiches	11

Breads & Brunch

Apple & Sausage Breakfast Bake	29
Apple Coffee Cake	22
Apple Nut Bread	18
Apple Pinwheel Rolls	24
Apple Scones	20
Apple-Blueberry Muffins	16
Apple-Cheese Bread	21
Apple-Zucchini Bread	19
Country Apple Biscuit Bake	23
Dutch Baby Apple Pancake	32
Fruit-Topped Baked Pancake	31
Ham & Apple Casserole	30
Mini Apple Muffins	14
Next Day A.M. Bread Pudding	26
Overnight Apple French Toast	28
Streusel-Topped Pumpkin Muffins	15
Sweet Apple Fritters	17
Whole Wheat Apple Pancakes	27
Yummy Apple Oatmeal	25

Salads & Sides

Apple & Rice Salad	49
Apple Coleslaw	43
Apple-Cheddar Toss	46
Apple-Citrus Salad	42